THE TULSA

MASSACRE OF 1921

The Worst Race Riot in American History

Matthew Williams

TABLE OF CONTENTS

CHAPTER ONE

THE EMBERS

D espite the role that he would play in history, very little is known about Jimmie Jones. Jones, being an orphan, and a black child, and a boy, did not start life easily. Orphans in the early 1900s were less likely to be adopted by a couple in need of a child as much as they were to be adopted by a farmer or landowners who wanted free labor. For non-white children, and for boys especially, the later was even more common. After all, most childless couples wanted to act as though the child they adopted was born from them. African American couples were often barred from adoption due to their race, leaving non-white children to be taken almost exclusively by people looking for free child labor. When Jimmie and his two sisters, for reasons unknown, wound up in an orphanage in Vinita, Oklahoma, in 1908, it is possible he believed that his fate would be one of hard farm work, or worse.

In a rare bit of luck, Damie Ford ne` Rowland, on her way home to the Greenwood District of Tulsa, Oklahoma, happened to stop by the orphanage where Jones lived. She was a smart woman and utilized stereotypes to her favor and, claiming to be family, informally adopted Jones. At the time of this writing, there are no documents that support a blood relation between Jones and Damie

Ford. She brought him home to Tulsa and raised him as her own. Jones changed his name after some years of living with Ford and her family. He became Dick Rowland. Rowland for his adopted mother, and Dick, a popular name for strong characters in the era.

Rowland, a child of segregated education, dropped out of Booker T. Washington High School in his teens and decided to take up shoe shining. He plied his trade on the Main Street of Tulsa, and, according to those who knew him, he made a decent enough living. By all accounts, he never got into the kind of trouble that would have wound up on a permanent record. He was well-liked in his community and was just one of thousands of Americans trying to make their way after World War I and the age of industrialization.

He was just a young man who shined shoes.

One Monday near the end of May, Rowland needed to use the bathroom. He could not use the one at the shop where he worked. Jim Crow laws were strict about who could use which bathrooms, and the facilities at his job were strictly for the all-white clientele, even though nearly all the employees were African American. Instead, due to an arrangement that the boss had with the nearby Drexel Building, Rowland and his coworkers were allowed to use the restrooms at the top of the building, which they could get to by elevator.

Sarah Page, according to what few records are available, was a native of Kansas City. She moved to Tulsa at 17 and was in the midst of getting a divorce. While divorce is common today, in 1921 it was rare and usually signified that the relationship had been abusive in some way. Divorced women had minimal income options, but Page was lucky that the Drexel Building had needed an elevator operator. In this era, weren't there to push buttons but manually operate the lever system and greet customers. She was working her shift on the day that Rowland stepped into the elevator to get to the bathroom. As they both worked a great deal, it would not be a stretch to say they had seen one another before.

According to Rowland, as he was entering the elevator, he tripped. He grabbed the first stable thing that was in arms reach. It just so happened to be the arm of one Sarah Page. The two of them stumbled back, and Page, startled, cried out.

Rowland ran.

A first floor clerk for the Drexel Building, whose name has been lost to time but was noted in reports as being white, called the police and reported the incident as an attempted assault, which, in those times, meant attempted rape.

Rowland was arrested within hours of the incident.

The headline "Nab Negro for Attacking Girl in Elevator" ran in the May 31st issue of the Tulsa Tribune. It exaggerated the incident until it sounded as if Page had been hit, and her clothing torn. The article goes on to say that Dick Rowland liked to call himself "Diamond Dick," making him out to be like some sinister comic book character. It mislabeled him as a delivery boy, claimed that she was helping police with Rowland's capture, and labels her as the orphan who was "working as an elevator operator to pay her way through college."

Almost none of this is true. Sarah Paige declined to press any charges. She wasn't an orphan. She was a teenage divorcee, which certainly wouldn't have made for good paper fodder. No documents say she had anything to do with Rowland's identification. It was the white clerk who helped in the arrest. If

3

Page ever had anything to say about the attack, it was drowned out in the clerks, journalists, and police officers who spoke for her.

Either way, Rowland was arrested by officers Carmichael and Pack and held to await his moment at the Municipal Court.

No one knows who started to spread the rumor of lynching. Some claim that white men and women were demanding it. Others say that black men and women were expecting it. The truth is probably somewhere between the two. In the history of the United States, there have been 4,743 documented lynchings; 73% of lynching victims were black. Of 1,297 white victims, nearly all of them were lynched for helping black men and women. The remaining few received this punishment for being "anti-lynching," domestic abusers, murderers, or cattle thieves.

Oklahoma fell outside of the norm of these statistics. In its history, there were 107 lynchings. Seventy-one were white, 17 were black, 14 were Native American (Indian on documentation), one was Chinese, and three were of unknown race. However, it should be noted that nearly all the white lynchings were done before 1907. After that, they took on a more race-driven overtone. By 1921, this form of mob justice often played out against African Americans. Black communities were especially aware of this, so when the rumor mill churned out the idea that the hundreds of men from the white community of Tulsa were ready to brand their own justice for the sake of little orphan Page, they came out to protect him.

Seventy-five black men, some who were armed, showed up at the prison to protect Rowland. There was no mob, just a sheriff, who promised that he had everything under control asked the men to disperse. They complied.

As the black men were leaving, a mob of white men arrived. According to some reports, the white men seemed most upset because the black men were armed. A debate took place, tensions rose. One unnamed white man attempted to disarm an armed black man. The gun went off and, according to the sheriff, "All hell broke loose."

When the dust finally settled, Tulsa would never be the same.

CHAPTER TWO

A HISTORY OF NATIVE AMERICANS, FREEDMEN, TULSA, AND GREENWOOD

I t is impossible to understand what happened in Greenwood without looking into the past. It was not an isolated incident. It was not uncommon. It could have been avoided. In order to understand the explosion, one must first get acquainted with the era. After all, what happened in Tulsa did not occur in a vacuum.

This history of Native Americans and African Americans is, in many ways, linked. While the rules about African Americans differed from one Native American tribe to the next, before the Civil War, many Native groups would take in runaway slaves either temporarily before sending them on their way, or permanently by integrating them into their tribe. In other circumstances, black slaves were sold to members of the wealthy Creek or Cherokee tribes.

In 1830, President Andrew Jackson, under pressure from the American Southeast, finished what George Washington started and signed the Indian Removal Act. It forced 60,000 Native Americans from their lands and into the American Southwest. This caused many problems for those who were either black or of mixed Native/African genetics. One drop of blood was enough to make someone "black" through much of history, and the laws for Native Americans were very, very different for African Americans. Each tribe had to decide what their rules were, and what the requirements of African Americans would be. Many tribes took to the Trail of Tears as broken families, leaving their African American relatives behind, or, in some cases, taking the children along, but leaving the "full black" parents behind. It made a messy situation already messier. For the Creek or Cherokee who owned black slaves, they were often forced to bring along their "possessions" or risk them being killed.

When the dust settled, Tulsa became the home of the Loachapoka, who fell under the Creek Nation, after being forcibly relocated from their native Alabama. It is entirely possible that people of African heritage were mixed into this group. One man, whose name has been lost to history, was described as being a short, muscular man of deep brown skin. The Loachapoka set a ceremonial fire beneath a burr oak tree that still stands in what is now called Creek Nation Council Oak Park, and dubbed their new home Tulasi, which means "old town." They would continue to use the burr oak as a place for festivals and ceremonies for about 70 years.

Sixteen years after the Loachapoka resettled, Lewis Perryman, who was part Creek Native and part white, built a log cabin just outside of the Loachapoka lands. He raised married a white woman, had at least three children, and sold cattle. The Civil War, which Perryman had no desire to take part in, came and went. Perryman traveled to Kansas to stay out of the conflicts and eventually died away from his ranch. Perryman's son built the first post office in the area and became its postmaster. More families moved into the area. They renamed Tulsi to Tulsy Town, and, under the Perrymans, became the most massive cattle operation in all of Creek Nation. They built stores, hotels, and with money born of cattle, they began to carve out little luxuries for themselves.

Northwest of Tulsy Town, O.W. Gurley bought 40 acres. Gurley was a black man, born and raised in Alabama. He was well educated and respected by blacks and whites alike. Grover Cleveland offered Gurley an appointment under his presidency, but Gurley decided to stake out a bit of land and start building his own community.

Freedom Towns had, to some degree, always existed. After the Native Americans had been pushed from lands, leaving black friends and family behind, there were sections of the American Midle, East, and Southwest that were overwhelmingly black. However, after the Emancipation Proclamation, and the Thirteenth Amendment, these areas grew not only in size but also in number. Gurley's 40 acres, which would become known as Greenwood, was one of these.

The land bought by Gurley was "only to be sold to Colored." This appealed to many freemen and former slaves. Racial tensions were still incredibly high in the Reconstruction Era, and, for many, it was decided that the best way to deal with this was to separate the races. Greenwood, as established by documentation, was for blacks and blacks only.

The Atlantic to Pacific railroad went through Tulsy Town and Greenwood, which meant different things for both. For Tulsy, the railroad was a way to move cattle, which was the core of their livelihood. For Greenwood, which had become a haven against persecution, it meant an opportunity for work. Gurley's first business at Greenwood was a rooming house, a multi-tenant house where people had separate rooms that they could rent for a few nights or even a few years but had shared bathing facilities. A church was built, small farms and homes were established. Slowly and steadily, Greenwood, like Tulsy, was starting to resemble a town.

Ten years after Gurley bought the 40 acres, another wealthy black man moved into the area. J.B Stradford was born to a former slave, who had been named Ceaser by his master. Ceaser was taught to read by his owner's daughter. He learned about the Emancipation Proclamation and petitioned for his freedom. He was eventually freed, and took the name Stradford as his own, and passed on everything that he knew to his children, especially his firstborn, J.B.

J.B Stradford, who got an education at Indiana University, supported freedom towns and thought that he could help them survive. His college years had taught him about history, social justice, and finances. In 1899, the same year that Tulsy Town, Greenwood, and several other smaller districts incorporated to officially become Tulsa, Oklahoma, Stradford moved into the area. He believed that black men and women would only be able to survive if they pooled their resources and offered constant support to one another. It worked.

Within a few years of reinvesting in Greenwood, Stradford became one of the wealthiest and most influential black men in the United States. The Stradford Hotel was the largest black-owned, black-operated, and black-guest only hotel in America. The hotel matched its white-owned counterparts by offering jazz music, comfortable living, gambling, and food. Flanked on either side were other businesses owned by wealthy and influential black men and women: restaurants, barbershops, tobacco and cigar shops, and more.

Because of Jim Crow laws, Greenwood was still separate from the other, white districts of Tulsa. Yes, it fell under the jurisdiction of Oklahoma, but it was where black men and women could own businesses, walk around freely, and rent property without fear. In Greenwood, African Americans could carve out their idea of the American Dream, and with the help of Stradford, they were thriving.

Not everyone thought that it was deserved.

CHAPTER THREE

THE FANNING OF THE FLAMES

———————◆———————

The Civil War and the Thirteenth Amendment freed black men and women but offered little recompense for their years of free labor. The war also left white Southern farmers with a lot of land, but no money to hire farmhands to tend it. The answer, in the beginning, was sharecropping. Popular in many parts of the world, sharecropping is a relatively simple practice. In exchange for a roof over their head, laborers (in the case of the American South, sharecroppers were former slaves) would work a section of land. At harvest, sharecroppers, instead of offering paper payment, would give a portion of the crops instead. Sharecroppers did not own their home, their tools, or the land. The only thing they had to sell was their crop. High tax rates to pay for the South's rebuilding meant that many farmers and sharecroppers had nothing to set aside for the following year at the end of the season. White landowners became frustrated with the situation and began selling off the land, leaving many black sharecroppers without land to work, or a home to live in.

One of the few exceptions to this was the cotton crop. Cotton, desperately needed across the entire country, was one of the few crops that could be grown at a profit, though a meager one, for everyone involved. Problems arose when taxes went up. Local laws set taxes. However, between Jim Crow laws, literacy tests, poll taxes, and grandfather clauses, many black sharecroppers and other non-whites living in the South were deemed unfit to vote. Therefore, sharecroppers were being taxed, but they weren't allowed to vote on those taxes.

And then, starting in 1914 and continuing through 1916, a boll weevil infestation took root, which turned an already tricky cycle into an impossible one. Desperate to leave bleak circumstances, newly free black men and women started The Great Migration.

Between 1914 and 1920, over 500,000 black men and women left the South. It is still the most significant population movement in the United States. They migrated primarily to the North and the American Southwest, seeking haven in districts like Greenwood. This created strain in the South, where the labor force dwindled by a third. But it also created pressure in the North and the Southwest, where suddenly there were 500,000 new people looking for work and places to live. The cities more affected by this Great Migration were Chicago, Cleveland, Detroit, New York, Pittsburgh, and Tulsa. In all of these cities, racial tensions arose. Whites, especially white men, felt that black men were taking jobs, and their families took up space. Black men were angry that white men were paid more for the same position, and that the places they could live under segregation were often inferior. Black men were accused of lewd and lascivious behavior towards white women. There are multiple instances of rape against a black woman by white men that went uninvestigated and unpunished. Both sides accused the other of taking things that they felt belonged to them.

In Little Rock, Arkansas, years before the Little Rock Nine would break segregation boundaries in education, the Little Rock Riots took place. It started in mid-September when Robert M. Mcdonald, a former police officer for the Argenta area of North Little Rock, killed a black musician, Wiley Shelby, in a barroom brawl. When a white coroner attempted to convene an inquest at a black-owned funeral home, tensions arose. They reached a breaking point when one of the funeral home workers, Robert Colum, attacked a white officer, Milton Lindsey, for refusing to let a group of black men onto the premises. A fight broke out, and two shots were fired. One of them killed Robert Colum on the spot. After a very brief investigation it was decided that Colum met his death "at the hands of someone unknown." This became a problem since many African Americans claimed that Lindsey was the only one to have fired.

In October, Milton Lindsey was walking with his father in front of the same funeral home andthe pair was shot. Elder Lindsey died from 11 gunshot wounds; Milton survived but was severely injured. When police officers attempted to enter the funeral home, they were fired. A mob of white men began to form. In an attempt to keep damage to a minimum, the mayor closed down the saloons and dismissed the right to bear arms for anyone but sworn officers. He also instituted a prohibition against anyone making "inflammatory statements." This may have caused more tension.

The black funeral directors and a black shoe salesman were charged with the murder of Elder Lindsey and the attempted murder of Officer Lindsey. However, the three men had escaped by the time the mob overtook the funeral home. Not finding their targets, the crowd set the home on fire and, according to several eyewitnesses, attempted to force black women and children back into the incinerating house.

Riots broke out. Buildings burned. People were shot. Some arrests were made, both black and white, but no one seemed happy about it.

All around the country, racial tensions rose and potentially fueled the riots in Atlanta, not even two weeks later.

In Atlanta, just like in Tulsa, pockets of freedmen attempted to build a life for themselves in the Reconstruction Era. Wealthy business owners were trying to push for political power, which was not welcome to many white business owners in the area. One of the most successful businesses was a barbershop owned by Alonzo Herndon, whose shop catered to white men of wealth. He and other black businessmen were gaining enough wealth and had enough education to overcome specific laws that had been implemented to keep the uneducated and the poor from voting. This caused fear in Democratic candidates, as well as the Democratic party, which at the time was closely aligned with the Ku Klux Klan. Smith, one of the candidates and a former editor for a popular newspaper, and Howell who was currently an editor for another newspaper used their journalistic connections to begin spreading misinformation about black-owned businesses in the hopes of decreasing their prominence and wealth, and thus make it more difficult for them to vote.

The papers made outrageous claims about the black-owned business, claiming that they were irreputable vice dens that posted lewd pictures of naked women on the walls. They referred to the saloons and other gathering places that were black owned as "dives" and made up reports about white women who were brutalized and raped by black men. They pushed for people to read "The Clansmen: A Historical Romance of the Ku Klux Klan." Stirred, angry, and fueled by inaccurate journalism, white men in large groups began walking the streets armed and prepared to protect their businesses and women from what the politically owned papers referred to as "savage Negroes." They targeted any black man they found, beating them, stabbing them, or shooting them. They focused on the Five Points section of downtown Atlanta, where streetcars often picked up or dropped off black men for work. It started with 500 men, and, by midnight, had swelled to over 15,000. Thousands of black men were assaulted, three were killed. The governor called in the Infantry, which added to the confusion and the anger.

Between midnight and 3 a.m., 30 more black men were killed, most by stabbing, several by gunshot, and a few through beatings. The streetcars had stopped running. With a lack of victims readily coming to them, the mob turned their attacks on black-owned businesses, specifically those targeted by the Democratic newspapers. The barbershop of Alonzo Herndon was the first to be set on fire. The black post office was next, and a few men who had been sitting on the steps were killed before it was set on fire. More men and businesses were targeted until about 3:45 a.m. when a sudden, heavy rain dispersed the crowd of now nearly 20,000 anger-fueled white men.

The riots were publicized the world over. Many black communities gathered for their protection. In Atlanta, when 250 men came together to disguise how they were going to protect themselves, police raided their gathering and arrested them for inciting to riot. When the mayor of Atlanta was asked why the white rioters hadn't been arrested, but an assembly of non-rioting black men had been, he said, "The best way to prevent a race riot depends entirely upon the cause. If your inquiry has anything to do with the present situation in Atlanta, then I would say the only remedy is to remove the cause. As long as the black brutes assault our white women, just so long will they be unceremoniously dealt with."

In the papers that first fueled the riots, a letter reprinted around the world said the following: "Separation of the races is the only radical solution of the negro problem in this country. There is nothing new about it. It was the Almighty who established the bounds of the habitation of the races. The negroes were brought here by compulsion; they should be induced to leave here by persuasion."

All across America, racial tensions worsened.

In Wahalak and Scooba Mississippi, in December of 1906, for reasons unknown, several white men began attacking black men and women in small conflicts. Twelve blacks and two whites were killed. The riots ended when the sheriff called for the state militia.

The Race Riots of the early 1900s primarily focused on whites killing and burning down black-owned buildings, but there were riots against the Greeks (who were not seen as white) and the Chinese and even indigenous men and women. In Bellingham, Washington, 500 white men, members of the Asiatic Exclusion League, attacked the homes of immigrants from South East Asia. The victims were primarily Sikhs but were misrepresented as Muslims by the newspapers. Authorities arrested the populations that were targeted for their safety. Still, when the riots were over, they had nowhere to go and eventually went to British Columbia to seek a new life.

16

The Springfield Race Riots, The Pittsburgh Riots, the Hells Canyon Massacre, the New Orleans Anti-Italian Riot, Willmington, Lake City, Greenwood, South Carolina, and more followed. Between 1887 and 1914, there were a total of 27 documented race-related riots in America. Most were led by white motivated "redeemers" who were proudly protecting the American country from blacks. Hundreds of black men and women died, many by lynching and even more had been beaten. Less than 20 whites were killed in the course of these riots. Almost none were arrested for the destruction of property, and only a handful were held accountable for murder.

CHAPTER FOUR

SCIENTIFIC RACISM

AND THE TALENTED TENTH

———————◆———————

While America was rioting, science was stirring the pot.

In 1883, nine years before Jim Crow laws were passed, Sir Frances Galton, a British scientist and second cousin to Charles Darwin, developed a theory. He had focused much of his academic life on the study of psychology (which was still finding its footing), of naturalism (the removal of romanticism from science in favor of social commentary, detachment from emotion, and scientific observation), and anthropometrics (the study of measuring parts of the body such as height and weight, as well as the measurements of the skull, ears, and length between joints). Sir Frances was regarded as a pioneer in many of these very young fields. His association with Darwin allotted his views some weight in a society that was moving away from emotion and focusing instead on what was considered logical.

Frances grew up hearing about Darwin's theories of evolution and "survival of the fittest." He also grew up hearing about racial differences. He was fascinated with what makes people different and how one can best ensure the birth of a superior human. And, for him, the superior human was white.

It is important to note that interracial relationships happened before the Jim Crow era. Biracial, termed mulatto, made up 2.65% of the American Census in 1900 and was underrepresented in both black and white communities. Interracial relationships were rare and frowned upon, especially in the cases of black men with white women, but they were not illegal. In some instances, the couple was harassed and, in extreme cases, killed. The idea of interracial relationships bothered people, white and black. Both saw this as a reduction of their own racial identity, but for different reasons. Whites seemed to be afraid that intermixing would make them lesser. Blacks seemed more afraid that intermixing would erase them.

Edward Ross popularized the term "Race Suicide" and firmly believed that comingling would create something lesser. According to Ross, "fit" women, which was defined by him as wealthy white women of Catholic or Protestant stock, who were mentally and physically capable did not have as many children as possible, to outbreed those who were "unfit" (anyone who wasn't white, anyone who wasn't Protestant or Catholic, and anyone who had a mental or physical illness that was deemed unsuitable) and therefore save the "superior race." Ross was not alone in his fears.

Theodore Roosevelt, who was a steadfast believer in Noridcism (the idea that Nordic races were the superior race but also endangered) during his presidency, was asked about his stance on racial suicide. He said during a 1902 speech that "(racial suicide is) fundamentally infinitely more important than any other question in this country." The next year he doubled down on his stance. He

19

said, "the man or woman who deliberately avoids marriage, and has a heart so cold as to know no passion and a brain so shallow and selfish as to dislike having children, is in effect a criminal against the (white) race, and should be an object of contemptuous abhorrence by all healthy people."

Their views and aversion to being childless by choice were born in Sir Frances' work.

In 1883 Sir Frances published a book, "Inquiries into the Human Faculty and its Development." In it, he proposes that there must be a scientific way to give "more suitable races" a way to ensure that they will "(prevail) speedily over less suitable races. He called this proposition "eugenics."

Eugenes, the term that Frances derived his theories from, means to come from good stock with desirable traits, to come into being, to grow. His concept was that through the genetic history of a person, we could define their potential, and by making sure that they could and did reproduce with equally good or better, create a superior offspring. People of wealth tend to be taller. People of intelligence have heads that are shaped a certain way. Disfigurements and mental weaknesses were not allowed to add to the genetic pool. It wasn't a matter of heart, he believed; it was, in his own words, "nature vs. nurture." That is a term that is still in use today, though often misunderstood and misused.

Like many in even today's pseudo-scientific circles, Sir Frances' idea of "survival of the fittest" was not understood or used correctly. Survival of the fittest did not mean that the strongest would survive any situation. According to Darwin, the creatures that best suited, or "fit," their natural environment. However, Sir Frances took his misinterpretation and created a pseudo-science that American and British scientists (both black and white) latched onto. Not only would this create more firmly rooted problems within America, but his work would also eventually be part of the fuel for World War II and Nazi ideas on race.

In America, however, almost 50 years before the rise of Adolph Hitler, eugenics created a deeper racial divide. Sir Frances' work was read by the educated elite and taught as pure science. The University of Virginia became the central home of the movement to create barriers between those who were fit and those who were not. Whites thought that they would be made lesser by mixing with African Americans, and African Americans felt that they would be erased by mixing with whites.

The problem, white eugenicists said, was not just social; it was political and financial, too. By mixing genetics, we allowed ourselves to become weaker in mind and the body. The superiority of the Nordic traits would be muddied and eventually vanish entirely, creating scores of mentally and physically unfit people who would become a drain on our country's financial resources.

Educated African Americans took Sir Frances' theories differently. It is unknown who came up with the idea of "the Talented Tenth," but it is a theory that many latched on to and spread throughout black communities. Some pamphlets link rhetoric for the Talented Tenth back to The American Baptist Home Mission Society, which was a white, liberal, Christian missionary that was attached to wealthy liberal whites such as John. D. Rockefeller. The missionary believed in educating blacks through black-centric colleges, especially in the South. Their goal was to train black educators. They had good intentions, but these intentions did not have the desired effect. One of the things that was taught was the Talented Tenth.

The Talented Tenth theory was the idea that one out of every 10 black men would have the ability to become leaders of their race. One of these educated elites was W.E.B Du Bois.

Du Bois was born in Massachusetts within a relatively liberal community that allowed for integration and racial tolerance. He attended the University of Berlin as well as Harvard and became the first African American to receive a doctorate. He was a professor, a scientist, an author, and considered himself to be one of the Talented Tenth. He spearheaded the Niagara Movement and was a founding member of the National Association for the Advancement of Colored People, commonly referred to as the NAACP. He, along with Booker T. Washington (another who Du Bois believed was a Talented Tenth), helped to create and pen the Atlanta Compromise, which proposed that Southern blacks would submit to the rule of the Southern whites, provided that whites would receive opportunities for education and advancement within their communities. Du Bois became a professor at the Atlanta University where he taught other African Americans about history, sociology, economics and preached racial uplift and eugenics.

In 1903, several African Americans penned and published a collection of essays known as "The Negro Problem." In Du Bois' submission, he pushes the idea of the Talented Tenth and claims "the Negro race, like all races, is going to be saved by its exceptional men. The problem of education, then, among Negroes must first of all deal with the Talented Tenth; it is the problem of developing the Best of this race that they may guide the Mass away from the contamination and death of the Worst." He believed that through these elite leaders, black communities would survive, but only if they focused their energy and attention on these elite few. He, like the mission, had good intentions, but they developed into something that he would vehemently oppose.

Eugenics, Nordicism, racial suicide, The Talented Tenth, and fear would be the bricks that would be used to develop Jim Crow laws. After all, if the fear was comingling, the best thing someone could do would be to keep the races separate, giving them the individual spaces they need to create the best representation of their own race.

Chapter Five

JIM CROW LAWS

---◆---

Thomas D. Rice was a white actor who traveled and performed across the United States. His minstrel show, which was the live action precursor to the televised variety show, was his first real success. Born in New York, Rice was primarily a stock player before he stumbled on the character who would eventually become known as Jim Crow.

The source material of Jim Crow has been lost, but it is known that Rice did not make the character up on his own. Jim Crow had been a character from slave stories, usually depicted as a wanderer. Rice took the idea, and perhaps some of the stories that have since been lost, and exaggerated them. Rice claimed he mimicked an actual slave that he came across, one who had a hunched back and a broken leg, who walked with a little hop and liked to sing as he worked. He even claimed that he bought the man's clothes to give the character more realism, but that has been hotly disputed by historians. It is not possible to know what is true.

What we are sure about is that Rice began playing the character of Jim Crow in the late 1820s, and made him his signature act by 1932. He was not the first actor to paint himself to look darker, a practice that would become known as blackface, but he was certainly the most popular. He would paint his face and exaggerate his lip size to emulate stereotypes of black features. Then, carrying a sack over one shoulder, Rice would hunch over and do a hobbled jump as he sang a song called "Me and My Shadow." A child, also white and dressed in black face, would pop out of the bag and comically attempt to mimic Rice's movements. As the character of Jim Crow, Rice would speak in hyperbolic slang, pretend to be submissive to a Master but angry and violent when the Master turned his back. He made fun of Andrew Jackson, who wanted to be president without coming from the batch of Northeastern Elites that the vast majority of the American politicians came from. Jim Crow was a liar, a thief, and a vagabond. He could not be trusted to work without someone constantly looking over his shoulder. He parodied Shakespeare, called slaves lazy, and performed these shows across America and into London. The character was, so far, the most popular representation of the African American slave in the era. So popular that the term Jim Crow became synonymous with "uneducated" and "negro," often at the same time.

And while many could argue that the character of Jim Crow was made in good fun, the fact that this name became the trademark for the laws that would legitimize segregation cannot be overlooked. By popularizing a caricature of slaves, his image would be used as a basis for legitimizing casual racism. It was easy to say that black men and women belonged in slavery when the most popular version of an enslaved black man was an uneducated man who would vote for a ridiculous leader if given the chance.

Jim Crow became the face of the enslaved, and it was not a great look.

Even after freedom was granted to African Americans, Jim Crow was the stereotype that persisted. A stereotype that African Americans, who had not been given the same educational privileges that whites had been afforded, were struggling to overcome. With race riots and eugenic theories pervading the country, it was only a matter of time before this character was used to push forward policies that would separate blacks and whites.

Rice died in 1860, and segregation laws began to take place shortly thereafter. Segregation laws did not happen overnight. They happened in bits and pieces, first in towns, and then in states. They were not laws that came into being without conflict, and in many cases with riots. Many historians say that the Wilmington Massacre was the lynchpin in the Reconstruction Era that lead to the Jim Crow Era. And, considering that Jim Crow Laws played a part in what would ultimately happen in Greenwood, it is important to discuss how those laws came to be.

Prior to 1870, Republicans were more liberal and spearheaded the anti-slavery mission. During the early years of the Reconstruction Era, they maintained a large portion of political offices in the south. During the late 1860s and early 1870s, Democrats would begin forcing their way into office, especially in the South.

In 1874 the White League, traditionally called the White Men's League, formed. The White Men's League was an insurgent paramilitary group that worked along with the Redshirts, who were one of the United States' first White Supremacist groups. Together, they used aggressive, often violent, intimidation tactics to force the outcome of voting. Republican candidates were forced to withdraw, run out of town, and in two cases, went missing. When blacks attempted to vote, they were often met with violence. Voter fraud was commonly used. Redshirts and men from the White Men's League would vote, change their clothes, go to a different polling station, and vote again. If they were questioned, they would often bully their way into voting anyway. It became a movement.

In areas where the intimidation tactics did not work, riots took place. In no place were things so obvious than in North Carolina. Wilmington, a port town prior to the Civil War, had been overwhelmingly black, with a large population of almost 10,000. Most of Wilmington's citizens worked the docks, but freedmen slowly became a large portion of the demographic. Freedmen operated as artisans and skilled laborers. With the end of the Civil War, and the creation of the Thirteenth and Fourteenth Amendments, Wilmington, like Greenwood, became a black community. Unsurprisingly, they also became largely Republican. This political position was not just because African freedmen were inclined to vote for the more liberal party, but because for a short period after the Civil War, Confederate veterans were barred from voting or holding office. Republicans pushed for the Ironclad Oath to become part of the swearing in ceremony of any public officer. The Oath went as follows:

I, NAME , do solemnly swear (or affirm) that I have never voluntarily borne arms against the United States since I have been a citizen thereof; that I have voluntarily given no aid, countenance, counsel, or encouragement to persons engaged in armed hostility thereto; that I have neither sought nor accepted nor attempted to exercise the functions of any office whatever, under any authority or pretended authority in hostility to the United States; that I have not yielded a voluntary support to any pretended government, authority, power or constitution within the United States, hostile or inimical thereto. And I do further swear (or affirm) that, to the best of my knowledge and ability, I will support and defend the Constitution of the United States, against all enemies, foreign and domestic; that I will bear true faith and allegiance to the same; that I take this obligation freely, without any mental reservation or purpose of evasion, and that I will well and faithfully discharge the duties of the office on which I am about to enter, so help me God.

Wilmington, whose biracial party was staunchly Republican, held strongly to this oath. They felt that anyone who had been part of the Confederacy was someone who had not only gone against the United States as a whole but was someone who had supported slavery.

Meanwhile, former Confederate soldiers felt disenfranchised. While there were plenty of soldiers who fought to keep slaves, many fought to protect their lands, were pressured under threats of violence by those who believed in the conflict more than they did, and men who weren't given a great deal of choice. It's important to note that slaveholders who had more than 20 slaves did not have to serve in the Confederate Army. When they failed to win, and in many cases failed to protect what they fought for, Confederate veterans became angry and looked for someone to blame. The Democratic Party was happy to point a finger at the Republicans in general, and upstart blacks specifically. Former Confederates became bitter at the lack of representation they had in politics and began joining organizations such as the Redshirts, the White League, and even the Ku Klux Klan.

In 1884, Ironclad Oaths are repealed, and the political climate of the South begins to shift. Under the banner of disenfranchisement, white-led organizations violently shifted the political climate of the American South. In Wilmington, the Redshirt movement began to bloom. Democrats looked for any way to unseat the Republican-dominated political system of the area, even attempting to abolish "home rule," which is the practice of local elections for local positions. Instead they wanted to make local political offices an appointment position from higher up the political chain, which is easier to control and manipulate.

In their continuing bid to take over Southern politics, Democrats, who were by this point largely made up of members of White Supremacist organizations, began to manipulate laws to work for whites and whites only. In North Carolina, things were especially bad. Through state judiciary systems, they drafted and pushed through 30 amendments to state constitutions. The North Carolina General Assembly removed offices that they couldn't manipulate, specifically judges of the state Supreme Court and for smaller areas who could stop their changing of the laws, and granted the area to the purview of something they controlled, usually the state legislature. They amended who could and could not vote specifically targeting crimes that were more likely to be committed by the black community, a tactic made easier by the fact that an overwhelming majority of law enforcement agencies in the South were also men from the White League and the Ku Klux Klan. White men who committed a crime that would have made them unable to cast a vote were let off with a warning, or a lighter sentence than a black man. Segregating public schools became mandatory, and since voter suppression was largely based on education levels, this made it easier to keep black men from voting. And, in nearly all states, they outlawed interracial relationships. Democrats also granted the General Assembly, which they controlled, the ability to nullify local government. In the Western part of the state, things were easier because they were predominately white, but in the largely black Eastern side of the state, tensions arose. It did not help that, as these changes took place, white Americans who believed in segregation and similar views began to move into the state, disrupting the demographics even further.

In 1876, the Democratic Party decided it was their time. They pushed for Zebulon Baird Vance, who had been a North Carolina governor during the Civil War and an owner of somewhere between 18 and 25 slaves, who made a bid for reelection now that he didn't have to take the Ironclad Oath. Vance ran on a platform of segregation and protecting former Confederate soldiers. He was staunchly against the platforms of the liberal Republicans and even called the Republican Party "begotten by a scalawag out of a mulatto and born in an outhouse." Democrats believed that they would win Vance back his seat and continue their eastward expansion.

But things didn't go exactly how they hoped.

Vance was also an expansionist. He believed that the best way to reinvigorate the South was to bring in big business and railroads. This became problematic for white North Carolina farmers who were already having a hard time making ends meet due to taxes and a dwindling affordable labor force. These farmers didn't want to be Republicans, but they no longer supported the business-minded Democrats either. They pulled their support from Vance and his party and created the Populist movement, sometimes referred to as The People's Movement. Their movement gained immense support during the Economic Depression of 1892 and banded together with black Republicans who, while they didn't have the same political views, believed that Vance was not what

North Carolina needed in this time. Together, they created the Fusion Coalition.

The population of Wilmington, which was seen as a haven for black men, swelled to 25,000, 55% of which were African American. There were black business owners, black educators, and black artisans. They were not only a demographic majority, they were also a fiscal majority, having taken the skills that they used in enslavement and creating businesses that accounted for 30% of Wilmington's monetary power. In an age of both overt racism and economic depression, this made them a target. Add on to this that a large amount of local political positions (deputy court clerk, justice of the peace, and street superintendent) as well as position of power (coroners, police officers, educators, and mail clerks, auctioneers, barbers, and architects) were black, the Democratic Party began to see Wilmington as everything that was wrong with the Republican Party. They declared an informal war against North Carolina's largest and most prosperous city.

Their first mode of attack was the tried and true use of journalism. Newspapers were one of the areas of business that was still predominately white, with the noted exception of the Wilmington Daily Record. The papers began to spew daily misinformation campaigns against black officials, targeting any African American who was in a position that could have gone to a white man. These papers were delivered to any organization or business that had found hard times in the hopes of stirring up poor whites. Unskilled whites were often jobless and needed someone to blame.

The tension can be summed up in two quotes from papers in the era:

"While thus numerically strong, the Negro is not a factor in the development of the city or section. With thirty years of freedom behind him and with an absolute equality of educational advantages with the whites, there is not today in Wilmington a single Negro savings bank or any other distinctively Negro educational or charitable institution; while the race has not produced a physician or lawyer of note. In other words, the Negro in Wilmington has progressed in very slight degree from the time when he was a slave. His condition can be summed up in a line. Of the taxes in the city of Wilmington and the county of New Hanover the whites pay 96 2/3rds per cent; while the Negroes pay the remainder — 3 1/3rds per cent. The Negro in North Carolina, as these figures show, is thriftless, improvident, does not accumulate money, and is not accounted a desirable citizen."

The Washington Post hoped that by pointing this information out (some of which is exaggerated to the point of inaccuracy) that the Democratic paper could lead people to believe that African Americans might have money, but they were not good with money, and therefore not good for government positions which demanded a certain amount of fiscal responsibility.

"An impression prevails that these colored people have grown greatly in wealth, that they have acquired homesteads, have become tax-payers and given great promise along these lines. It is not true. In North Carolina they had as fair a chance as in any other Southern State – perhaps better than any other. And here it is sad to hear their frequent boast that they own eight millions of property. This is about three percent, according to the tax list, the total of which shows an amount much less than the actual total values of the State, but this fact does not disturb the proportion between the races. They are thirty percent of the population. After thirty years of opportunity, they have three percent of the property. True, they may claim that this is all net gain as they started with no property. But they did not

32

start with nothing. They started with enormous advantages over whites. They were accustomed to labor. The whites were not. They had been for generations the producers of the State and the whites the consumers. They were accustomed to hardship and privation and patient industry. They had the muscle. If in this thirty years they have only acquired this pittance, where will they be in another thirty years considering that the advantages of their start are largely, if not entirely lost?"

These words, spoken by Daniel L. Russel, who had also been a governor of North Carolina, wanted to show that blacks had been given an opportunity but hadn't made the most of it, and that perhaps their squander is what was leading into the current financial problems within the country. The papers went further to talk about the black-dominated Republican Party of Wilmington (despite the fact that the party was one-third black, despite the population of Wilmington being more than half black) was ruining the state as a whole to make way for "Negro Domination." They started drafting up false stories of white women being attacked by black men.

"Of all the threats a farm wife faces, none is greater than that of the Black Rapist," suffragette Rebecca L. Felton claimed in one newspaper. And she blamed white men for not keeping them safe. "When there is not enough religion in the pulpit to organize a crusade against sin; nor justice in the court house to promptly punish crime; nor manhood enough in the nation to put a sheltering arm about innocence and virtue – if it needs lynching to protect woman's dearest possession from the ravening human beasts – then I say lynch, a thousand times a week if necessary."

Her words caused many North Carolina men to join the Redshirt movement, which claimed to protect white women from black men. The acclaimed orator Alfred M. Waddell lent his voice to the movement. Waddell characterized himself as "the voice of the oppressed white" and, as a former member of politics and a wealthy white businessman, knew how to appeal to those who saw themselves as disenfranchised.

Three hundred Redshirts accompanied 22 "virtuous white women" in a parade around Wilmington to show that they were the only way a woman could walk around the predominately black city and not be accosted.

What few black papers there were claimed that black men weren't raping white women, but that consensual interracial relationships, some which had started before the laws against black and white relationships, were being framed as rape or sexual enslavement.

"We suggest that the whites guard their women more closely, as Mrs. Felton says, thus giving no opportunity for the human fiend, be he white or black. You leave your goods out of doors and then complain because they are taken away. Poor white men are careless in the matter of protecting their women, especially on the farms. They are careless of their conduct toward them and our experience teaches us that the women of that race are not any more particular in the matter of clandestine meetings with colored men than are the white men with colored women. Meetings of this kind go on for some time until the woman's infatuation, or the man's boldness, bring attention to them, and the man is lynched for rape. Every Negro lynched is called a "big burly, black brute", when in fact many ... were sufficiently attractive for white girls of culture and refinement to fall in love with them as is very well known to all."

That was the claim of Alexander Manly, writer and editor for the city's only black owned newspaper. He also noted that a black man would be lynched for raping a white woman. But a white man could rape a black woman and get away with it. His words stirred feelings in many on both sides, for different reasons.

The White Government Union, another White Supremacy group that called itself a club, pushed for every white man in Wilmington to join their ranks. They told white men that by electing them, they would be able to get the jobs that African Americans were stealing. They even held an event called the "White Supremacy Convention."

"The Anglo Saxon planted civilization on this continent and wherever this race has been in conflict with another race, it has asserted its supremacy and either conquered or exterminated the foe. This great race has carried the Bible in one hand and the sword. Resist our march of progress and civilization and we will wipe you off the face of the earth," the mayor of Durham claimed at this convention.

Things in Wilmington grew worse, and more complicated. Vance was elected. The number of White Supremacy groups swelled. Black businesses were targeted with acts of defilement and aggression. Laws became more crippling for African Americans, and lynching numbers reached an all-time high. Wilmington was a simmering pot of racial tension that was ready to boil over. The Fusionists and the Republicans did not want to give up their positions or their power out of fear of what might happen to over half the population of Wilmington. The Democrats, some of whom wanted to reinstate forms of legal slavery, and some of whom were disenfranchised with their lot in life, would take power through force if needed.

The entire town looked on the election with trepidation. The Post ran articles warning blacks to stay home. Large gatherings of Redshirts and Ku Klux Klan members happened in the city of Wilmington and in surrounding towns. Blacks and white Fusionists were afraid for their lives. No surprise as Congressman Kitchin said, "Before we allow the Negroes to control this state as they do now, we will kill enough of them that there will not be enough left to bury them." and, to stir emotions even hotter, Waddell followed Kitchin's words with the direction, "(citizens should) choke the Cape Fear with carcasses if necessary, to keep the Negroes from the poles."

Redshirts patrolled the roads to and from polling stations on horseback, some of them even wearing their Confederate uniforms. Many black businesses shut down for the day.

Democrats won every legislative seat in that election by a landslide. However, the number of votes superseded the population of the city, which shows that even if Fusionists had been allowed to vote, voter fraud would have silenced them anyway.

Many believed that the violence would ease or at least disappear until the newly elected Democratic Party could pass or revoke legislation that they desired. This is not how things went.

Once the election was over, Waddell, the speaker for the angry Democrats, led as few as 800 and as many as 2,000 white men to the capitol building. It was not enough that their political party had won the legislative seats. The local government still had three black men among them. Weddell and his men produced a document called "White Declaration of Independence" which stated: "We, the undersigned citizens… do hereby declare that we will no longer be ruled, and will never again be ruled by men of African origin." Now that the Democrats had power, they wanted to force the legitimate public servants out of their positions.

The following day, November 10, 1898, Waddell led 2,000 men to the Daily Record, Manly's black-owned newspaper, and burned it to the ground. Down the street, a group of black men, who were unarmed according to witnesses, came out of a black-owned grocery store. White men outside of a local saloon began to argue, and a gun went off. Someone shouted that a "white man killed." The pot of racial tension boiled over.

The 2,00 men, who were armed and ready to fight, tore through black neighborhoods, directed by the new Democratic government. Redshirts, like cavalry, rode through the streets, shooting unarmed black men. Men from the White Government Union marched through streets, looking for anyone who dared speak up against their actions. The Light Infantry, now under the direction of the Democrats, brought in a Gatling gun and used it on civilians. Their goal was to run off the black public servants, and, if they would not be intimidated, to kill them. Black officers and firefighters were "arrested for their own safety." That evening, those who were arrested were forcibly put on trains, with or without their family, and sent out of town. The police chief was forced to resign at gunpoint and a Democratic man was put into his place without an election. The now empty seats of the city council were replaced with men from the White League. Eighty men died, thousands were hospitalized, and 6,000 were left without a home to return to.

The newly installed political positions "elected" Waddell to the position of mayor.

What happened in Wilmington radiated across the state. Black-owned newspapers were doused in kerosene and set aflame. Black men and women who stood against these riots were arrested, beaten, or lynched. North Carolina fell to the rule of a political party largely made up of former Confederates. The South quickly followed suit.

The Wilmington Massacre remains the only coup d'etat on American soil, and it was the domino that led to the Jim Crow Era. Waddell and Vance led the way in writing and passing some of the harshest laws on segregation. The positions of power that they had taken during the massacre passed from one person from the White League to the next until many law officers, sheriffs, firefighters, councilmen and politicians in the South came from the KKK, the Redshirts, and similar White Supremacy groups. This would continue for years, and in some places has not changed.

CHAPTER SIX

WORLD WAR I

———————◆———————

Woodrow Wilson won his presidency by promising to keep the United States out of World War I, which was known at the time as The Great War. America was, according to most Americans, dealing with enough problems within its borders, problems that had been building for many, many years. Jim Crow laws, the riots that preceded them, and the problems that followed trying to maintain the often false concept of "separate but equal" was a slow burning war of the South. The North was dealing with the aftermath of The Great Migration, labor strikes, and the budding suffragette movement; and the South was handling the long term ripple of Wilmington, North Carolina, that found its way into Tulsa, which adopted the harsher version of the Jim Crow laws. Between 1889 to just a year after the Wilmington Massacre, Tulsa began to implement "separate but equal" policies around Oklahoma. In some cases, black neighborhoods were run out by members of white-centric groups, often at the prompting of the Confederate-run Democratic party. In places where African Americans would not willingly leave or rearrange their living to be separated from white areas, they faced violence and destruction of property to prompt forcible relocation. Across America, and especially in the South, those who did not give in to the steadily growing laws about segregation were forced to.

Lynchings against African Americans were at an all-time high. Between 1900 and 1915, Henryetta, Okemah, Purcell, Chickasha, Eufaula, and Oklahoma City all were the sites of public lynchings at the hands of white mobs. The victims were nearly always male.

The vast majority of America wanted to deal with the problems within the country's own borders rather than the ones that were happening across an ocean. United States citizens believed that they were immune to the effects of World War I and that getting involved would cause more problems than it would solve.

However, America's dislike for Germany grew over time. Long before Hitler and Nazis entered the picture, Germans were characterized as round faced and aggressive. Moments such as the "rape of Belgium" when the neutral country of Belgium was invaded and occupied by German troops, and the sinking of the Lusitania, a civilian passenger ship, by a Germany U-Boat began to sway public opinion against Germany. Day by day more American citizens began to ask why we were not doing something about the overt aggression of the German forces, and what would happen to us if they won? Britain put pressure on America as well. But America did not officially enter the war until American merchant ships met the same fate as the Lusitania, and the publication of the Zimmerman Telegram. The Telegram was a missive between Germany and Mexico, wherein Germany promised to help Mexico regain lost territories if they would help Germany in the war. To many this seemed like Germany planned on invading America as soon as it was done with Europe.

The Zimmerman Telegram spoke to many African Americans, as many of the remaining all-black communities had previously belonged to lands that had been part of Mexico. Many African Americans feared that if America did nothing about the Germans they would, yet again, be sent to live somewhere else, or forced to live under a political government that wouldn't see them as anything but second-class citizens.

This was not a universal fear. Some African Americans felt that Mexico may very well be a new chance. After all, the American government had done little about the White League and the Ku Klux Klan, which continued to cause problems within black communities. They wondered if maybe the Mexico might be a better option.

On April 2, twice-elected President Woodrow Wilson made an impassioned speech in front of Congress.

"I am not now thinking of the loss of property involved, immense and serious as that is, but only of the wanton and wholesale destruction of the lives of noncombatants, men, women, and children, engaged in pursuits which have always, even in the darkest periods of modern history, been deemed innocent and legitimate. Property can be paid for; the lives of peaceful and innocent people can not be. The present German submarine warfare against commerce is a warfare against mankind.

It is a war against all nations. American ships have been sunk, American lives taken, in ways which it has stirred us very deeply to learn of, but the ships and people of other neutral and friendly nations have been sunk and overwhelmed in the waters in the same way. There has been no discrimination. The challenge is to all mankind. Each nation must decide for itself how it will meet it. The choice we make for ourselves must be made with a moderation of counsel and a temperateness of judgment befitting our character and our motives as a nation. We must put excited feeling away. Our motive will not be revenge or the victorious assertion of the physical might of the nation, but only the vindication of right, of human right, of which we are only a single champion."

His words struck home for many, and pro-war group numbers surged. They parroted many of Wilson's sentiments, stating that if America did nothing they would be just as bad as the Germans. The world, they said, must be made safe for democracy.

These words were a powerful force in African American communities. After all, they knew better than nearly anyone within American borders what it felt like to have a taste of democracy and then have it taken away. They hoped that America would, inspired by the idea of "true democracy," see the war as a mirror of political reflection. After all, how could Americans fight for democracy in Germany, without giving its own citizens the very rights that they were willing to die for?

Black presses, far fewer in number but still politically active, were very vocal, though their opinions were not universal across black communities.

"If America truly understands the functions of democracy and justice, she must know that she must begin to promote democracy and justice at home first of all. Let us have a real democracy for the United States and then we can advise a house cleaning over on the other side of the water," Arthur Shaw, Baltimore *Afro-American*.

A. Philip Randolph and Chandler Owen, editors of the radical socialist newspaper *The Messenger*, stated over and over again that the democratic contract of freedom and equality had been unfairly applied to African Americans who did not have the same rights as whites, and therefore should not be part of the Draft. They felt that Germany had never, and could never, do to the black man what the American government already had. "The Germans ain't done nothin' to me, and if they have, I forgive 'em," was a popular expression around Harlem.

Even after America's official entry into World War I, which happened directly after Wilson's speech, there were plenty of groups, black and white, that felt America needed to stay out of the war. However, the June 1917 Espionage Act and the May 1918 Sedition Act went a long way to making sure that any anti-war protests were very quiet and swiftly dealt with. If a citizen was not pro-war, then they were anti-American, which was a dangerous thing to be.

The Draft, or the Selective Service Act of 1917, was an authorization by the government to raise an Army with the intent of sending them overseas to fight the Germans. Prior to 1917 the American Army was not particularly large. The Regulars, or the Regular Army, had just over 90,000 men. Organized state militias had 115,000 altogether. Wilson declared, shortly after the start of the war, that America needed 1 million soldiers. He got 73,000 volunteers. Therefore, the Draft was instituted.

The 1917 Draft required all men between the ages of 18 and 30 to register for potential military service. A year and a half later, the Draft was amended to include men up to the age of 45. This effort differed from previous ones, specifically that of the Civil War, by not allowing substitutions. That is someone could not serve in the place of someone else. If a man was called into service, and he was able of body, he must go into service. This was done to keep wealthy men from paying poorer ones to take their place. However, this was an inaccurate perception. While wealthy men would pay to keep themselves from service, they had the ability to commute service through a fee, which was often a cheaper option than paying for a substitute. Substitution was often used by "jumpers" or people who would offer their services as a soldier to families who did not want a family member to go to war. Jumpers, a form of conman, would take a fee, usually of hundreds of dollars and sign up as a substitute for the drafted member. Then they would desert before being sent anywhere. The lack of allowing substitutions hurt poorer town and neighborhoods more than it helped them.

If people were hoping that having an external enemy to focus on would quell the riots at home, they were wrong.

World War I helped solve a problem in American labor. A large portion of people who could fill a labor position had either volunteered or been drafted, leaving a vacuum of potential employment opportunities. St. Louis had a massive meat packing district, stockyards, and a surprising amount of metal fabrication shops; Aluminum Ore Co., American Steel Foundry, Republic Iron & Steel, Obear-Nester Glass and Elliot Frog & Switch to name a few. According to local sources, blacks were arriving in St. Louis at a rate of 2,000 per week. African Americans were often willing (or forced) to work at lower rates than their white counterparts and were thus hired more frequently. White laborers, already striking for fair and better business practices, saw the black laborers as enemies. Small squabbles broke out between the two groups that were often violent, but rarely lethal.

On July 2 1917, the steadily growing tensions between white laborers and black laborers reached a climax. Mobs of white men attacked black men over a period of four days. Over 100 black men were killed, though it is difficult to track down an exact number. It is known that eight white men were killed, their names were available in newspapers in the days following the violent breakout.

In Houston, something similar happened.

Camp Logan was a relatively new military base. New enough, in fact, that it was not even finished with construction when the Third Battalion of the 24th United States Infantry Regiment was ordered to its location to act as guards. They arrived with seven commissioned officers on July 27 1917, less than four months after America's entry into the Great War.

This caused a great deal of problems. The American Army was, like most of the country, segregated. The 24th was a black unit. Harris County, where the unfinished base was located, was a predominately white community. They saw the armed black soldiers in their county as an infiltration, especially the white construction workers who did not approve of sharing facilities with black men, regardless of a uniform. There were incidents involving the black soldiers and white law enforcement. A particularly difficult incident involved several soldiers playing a card game in the black area of the community and two officers breaking it up. The soldiers attempted to elude the police, and, in an attempt to find them, one of the officers dragged a black woman out onto the street. The soldiers were eventually sound, beaten, and arrested.

Word reached the 24th about what had happened, though they were not sure if the soldiers had been arrested or killed. The soldiers began to plan an attack on the local police force. One of the officers brought the prisoner back from the police station, which quieted issues somewhat. Even so, commissioned officers attempted to keep the peace by revoking passes and remanding the soldiers to base.

A white mob attempted to approach the base, and soldiers fired on them. A miniature war broke out between black soldiers and white police officers. Gunfire happened on both sides. Sixteen white civilians died, half of whom were law enforcement. Four black soldiers died. Court marshals were declared against 110 black soldiers. Sixty-three soldiers received life sentences for their participation in the riot, despite the fact that not all of them carried out lethal and 13 were hung without the American right of due process. Therefore, more black soldiers died than whites in Houston. Their bodies are still buried in unmarked graves.

Many newspapers framed what was deemed the Houston Mutiny as a reason why black soldiers could not be trusted.

Even so, black men continued to be drafted. The NAACP and W. E. B DuBois pushed for there to be more black leaders. They maintained that what happened in Houston would never have happened if there had been more black men in leadership positions rather than allowing white men to enforce themselves upon black soldiers. They declared that by having only white commissioned officers, America was reframing slavery. Black men did not have the right to turn down military service, and they were always put under a white officer/master. In an unprecedented move, they pushed men from black colleges to sign up to be officers. Over 1,200 showed up. They were trained at a camp in Des Moines, Iowa. At the end of the camp, 639 black men became some of the first black commissioned officers in the United States.

There were two divisions of all-black units: the 92nd division and the 93rd. Most of these soldiers were not sent to war, but rather put to work as laborers. This was a choice that had many pros and cons. On the one hand, it framed black men as good for nothing but hard work, and many of the forts that provided labor to the war effort were located in the American South. However, it did mean that, at least in the beginning of the war effort, many African Americans were not killed in combat duty. While black soldiers often received substandard uniforms, housing arrangements, and food, they also received access to health care and parts of the world they might have seen before. This was not welcomed by many white citizens who wondered why they had to send their sons to die overseas while black soldiers remained safely within our borders.

Racism was not exclusive to America. West African forces were called "naturally warlike" by the French elites and refused to allow African soldiers to receive the same awards and merits for similar acts within the French forces. In some circumstances the African forces were likened to the Germans, which created problems within many regiments. In many ways, the first World War was a war not just against Germany, but about racism on a global scale.

In the later years of the war, either by social pressure or through necessity, African American soldiers were sent to fight overseas. The 93rd was loaned out to the French, which, considering the French view of Africans, was probably was not the best choice. Even so, the 93rd did exceptionally well on the front lines. They were nicknamed the "Harlem Hellfighters" even though not all of those serving were from Harlem. Over 191 days the soldiers, who were put to the test, gave no land away to German forces. They were viewed as heroes and two of their number became the first non-white soldiers to receive the French War Cross. The French commoners, whose country had been ravaged by a war that had been pushed for by the French elite, welcomed the 93rd. The Harlem Hellfighters brought not just soldiers, but music and stories that they had not been exposed to. Their presence changed France for the years during and following the war.

The 92nd Division did not have a similar experience. Many of the members received ill treatment due to their race. Women were warned that African American men were prone to brutality and rape. Multiple charges were brought up against soldiers to get them dismissed from service or moved to different units. When one unit, the 368th, performed poorly, it was used as a testament of the poor ability of all black soldiers, rather than just a single instance of failure.

The 92nd expected to come home to a cold welcome; the 93rd, who had been treated as heroes, did not. "(The French civilians" treated us with respect, not like the white American soldiers." It created a strange cultural miasma in a post-armistice America.

It is no secret that all the soldiers, regardless of their race, experienced the atrocities of the Great War. A new form of mental illness, referred to as "shell shock" but called PTSD in modern times, began to rear its ugly head. Men, whether they were treated as heroes or not, returned home changed. Former soldiers were noted as "having a shaking of the limbs," deafness, bizarre sleep schedules, disassociation hallucinations, nightmares, ennui, depression, anxiety, strange gaits, eating disorders, violent outbursts, and an overwhelming sense of perpetual dread. This did not make it easy for many of them to find a place for themselves in the world that they helped create and maintain, and it was even more difficult for black soldiers who were, in many cases, returned home to a country that saw the failures of a few soldiers as the failures of all. Black soldiers had been talked into supporting the war by being told that their patriotic duty and their sacrifice would be a step forward for all African Americans.

W. E. B. Du Bois said the following:

"We return. We return from fighting. We return fighting. Make way for Democracy! We saved it in France, and by the Great Jehovah, we will save it in the United States of America, or know the reason why."

And yet, the Bloody Summer of 1919 proved that, soldiers or not, patriots or not, racism was still very much alive in the United States, and that the government was only going to do so much to help. Post-World War I America saw a boom in Ku Klux Klan numbers, and they were not relegated only to the South. In the years following Reconstruction, the KKK had become few in number, but during and after World War I the few thousand remaining swelled to over 100,000 active members, with passive support from people who were scared of the new changes that were spreading across America.

Jazz music, which was born from African American music traditions, became the music of the era, which many white Protestants saw as a gateway to vice and sin. Industrialization and mass production meant that many small town farmers could not afford the tools they would need to keep up with bigger, more elites farms, which would directly affect the South that had only just been finding its footing again. Urbanization became synonymous with poor and unwanted. The Suffragette movement was awarded the vote in 1920, which not only offered women a political voice, but a form of autonomy. Divorce numbers rose. Movies, radio, and national sporting events were beginning to be played in cities across the country, making the world seem smaller than before and more interconnected. There was a surge of immigration as people from countries torn apart by the Great War came to America, which promised a fresh start. Catholics, Jews, and anyone of "liberal persuasion" was seen as a threat to the predominately Protestant, conservative South. "Birth of a Nation," whose production and release could make a story in and of itself, was a film based on "The Clansman," the very book that had caused so many problems for African Americans during the Reconstruction, reimagined and spread across the entire country. The KKK framed their movement as traditionalist; "Truly American" would be the battle cry of anyone who was afraid of or uncomfortable with this new, post-war America.

Former soldiers, especially black men, had seen parts of the world where racial issues were not erased, but far less overt than they were in the land of the free. White soldiers brought back stories of European blacks who had positions of privilege and power under Marxist beliefs. Black soldiers, who had been heralded as heroes were forced back into the frame of second-class citizens, referred to themselves as "awakened" and that they could not go back to sleep. Whites, especially those in the South, saw this as a battle cry of the unreliable, potentially violent, shell shocked black soldier.

"The New Negro" was the idea that now that black men had seen the world, and what their lives could be they would return home and bring those ideas with them. The American fear was Bolshevism, or far-left radical views about labor, freedom, and Marxism being brought to American soil.

Fear, pushed by the still conservative Democratic Party and the swelling numbers of the KKK, stirred up not-so-old hatred, and race riots occurred across the United States in 1919. Hundreds of black men and women were killed, numerous were lynched. Specific numbers are impossible to get. Dozens of towns saw riots, lynchings, beatings, rapes, and murders done against black men and women. Due to the fact that an overwhelming majority of law enforcement was Protestant, conservative, and in many cases card-carrying members of the KKK, little was done about this. However, in the few circumstances where black men and women stood up against this, justice was swift, and often at the hands of the mob rather than the courtroom.

CHAPTER SEVEN

TULSA, BEFORE THE MASSACRE

———————◆———————

Experts on the Tulsa Massacre agree that there were several prior incidents that fed into what would happen on that Memorial Day in 1921. These incidents are not taught in casual history, and overall their importance seems small. However, that they happened at all gives validity to the fact that the social climate of Tulsa was reaching dangerous temperatures.

America was trying to rediscover itself after World War I. Movies, novels, and articles were all struggling to tell the story of a changing America, one that had more factories than farms and had a level of interconnectedness through radio and mass production that had not been seen before. Groups of men, black and white, who were being forced to work 16- and 20-hour shifts were fighting against oil barons who threatened to replace them with "cheaper blacks and immigrants." Women were learning how to live in a world where they could vote and potentially own their own property and businesses. War veterans were struggling with mental health and coming back to a country that had made them heroes overseas, and just another back to break in the warehouse.

Labor riots — strikes against overworking and underpaying — were common. They were not looked well upon by newspapers (often owned by wealthy businessmen) which thought that these men should be grateful to have a job at all. Unions were beginning to gain a foothold and power, pushing for the 40-hour work week and better pay. The Industrial Workers of the World was one of these unions and a heavy hitter in Tulsa's work force.

On October 29, 2017, J. Edgar Pew, one of the oil barons, discovered a bomb sitting on his front porch. It went off, though no one was injured. E. L. Lucas, the Tulsa police chief at the time, was quoted as saying it was a "gigantic plot to destroy the property of the oil companies and the residences of the leaders in the oil business."

The Tulsa World was one of Tulsa's newspapers at the time. It was staunchly antiunion and ran stories that implicated the IWW. It was the claim of Tulsa World that a source had said that the IWW were to blame. Several stories were run that stirred up antiunion causes, especially against the IWW. They claimed that the recent alliance between the IWW and a local chapter of the Oil Field Workers Union pitted both groups against wealthy oil tycoons. Under pressure from the newspaper, and J. Edgar Pew, police officers raided the headquarters of the IWW. They found 11 members of the union playing cards, eating lunch, and reading. They were charged and jailed for vagrancy.

The Tulsa World, bolstered by the arrests, began a media campaign against the 11 arrestees. They called the IWW traitors to America and the biggest threat to capitalism. "Get Out the Hemp," one headline read, and the paper called for the IWW members to be killed. At the trial, the arrested members said that they had joined the IWW to rally together for better wages.

T. D. Evans, the judge, did not accept this. Without much in the way of actual evidence, and the articles written by Tulsa World being cited periodically in place of facts, the judge not only declared the 11 men to be guilty, but decided that five supposed witnesses were to be arrested and found guilty as well. All of them were sentenced to jail.

While law enforcement was escorting these men to the jailhouse to begin serving out their sentence, 40 men clad in black robes who referred to themselves as the Sons of Liberty – a name that was used by anti-slavery organizations that helped free slaves before and during the Civil War — forcibly coerced the cops into giving up the convicted union members. The 40 men took the IWW members to a ravine, tied them to trees, whipped, tared, and feathered them. The IWW members, all of whom were white, were told never to return.

The Tulsa World referred to the Knights of Liberty, who had no association with the former slave freers, as a patriotic. It was an offshoot of the KKK that had formed shortly before World War I. The Tulsa chapter was largely made up of white business owners who were upset about Greenwood, many of them founding family members.

This shifted the view of vigilante justice in Tulsa. It was not just condoned; it was seen as a true heroic gesture.

In 1920 there were 61 lynchings. In 1921 there were 64. While the overwhelming majority of lynching victims were black men, several were white men. Two of the lynchings in 1920 happened in a single weekend, and these directly fed into the energy of the city that would ultimately lead to the burning of Black Wall Street.

On August 21, 1920, Home Nida got into his taxi for a shift of driving people around Tulsa. Nida was 25, and while he wasn't wealthy, he made a decent living. Partway through his shift he picked up a man and a woman. They were young. The woman, who remains unnamed, was said to have been in her late teens. The man, was 19-year-old Roy Belton. Belton used to be a telephone worker but had fallen on hard times and turned to drifting. He attempted to rob the taxi driver with a revolver.

Belton claimed the gun went off on accident. It did not matter. Nida was still dead.

Tulsa got riled up again. It is unknown exactly what caused the mob to form, but they got their hands on Roy Belton and lynched him from a sign. Several people said he ought to be shot, since he shot Nida, but it was decided that hanging was a more brutal, and therefore more acceptable, death.

The Tulsa police chief stated that while he did not condone mob law, the lynching of Belton was a good thing for their community. The sheriff, the mayor, and newspapers agreed with the sentiment.

Mob justice, vigilante justice, was exalted in Tulsa.

The day after Belton's lynching, Claude Chandler, a moonshiner who was accused of shooting two officers and wounding a third, was found hanging from a tree. He had been shot twice. Newspapers said that the African American community should have protected him from mob justice, and not to blame the officers for what happened to him.

Less than eight months later, Dick Rowland walked into the Drexel Building.

CHAPTER EIGHT

DICK ROWLAND'S FALL

---◆---

Monday, May 30, 1921. It is only three short years after the Red Summer. Jim Crow laws, even more enforced now than they were in previous years thanks to the resurgence of the KKK and other White Supremacist groups, keep blacks separate from whites in a bid to preserve racial purity, property values, and protect white women. While these laws were often framed as "separate but equal," a phrase given to the country through the landmark Plessy v. Ferguson case, there is very little evidence to support the idea that there was anything equal about it. When censuses were taken, it became clear that most African American communities lacked in health care options, in high education (and in some cases had no access to education at all), in business and employment opportunities, and religious availability. In places where black communities had these things, they were rarely as well funded as their white counterparts. In the South, and even sometimes in the North, these black-centric locations were targets of vitriol and racism. In many places, racial tensions were so fraught that people were looking for any reason to fight.

This is the world that Dick Rowland and Sarah Page grew up in. Rowland had been taught that education was for the whites and the wealthy. He had been told that he needed to stay away from whites, and from white women especially. Black men had been killed under the assumption that he had laid improper hands on a white woman. He had been told that jazz music, a product of his people, was a corrupting force causing women to have loose behavior and men to turn violent. With few options available to him, it is no surprise that the once orphan decided that finishing school wasn't worth his time; employment was. Shining white men's shoes was a better life choice for a 19-year-old black man than getting an education. His status was made clear when he had to leave his place of employment, walk across the street, get into an elevator, and travel up a building, past all the shops he wasn't allowed in, to get to a bathroom where he could do his business without being a problem the white citizens of Tulsa, Oklahoma.

And Page grew up in Kansas hearing about black men who raped white women. How much she believed this is unclear. However, considering that she was 17, had run from Kansas to Tulsa, and was seeking a divorce in an era where marriage was by and large till death do us part, that says that she wasn't weak. Even so, maybe she did scream when a 19-year-old black boy grabbed her arm. Many women would, regardless of the man's skin color. And, if statistics from the 1920s are to be believed, there is a good chance that Page was running from someone who put hands on her regularly. She never said so; in fact, she never said much at all.

So there Dick Rowland was, 19 years old, smelling of shoe-shine, and needing to use the restroom. With everyone wanting to look their best for Memorial Day, he had probably been bent over shoes all day. He informed his unnamed boss that he was headed over to 319 S. Main St., the Drexel Building, for a quick break. Or perhaps he was sent. Either way he crossed the street, busy with people who were looking for a way to honor soldiers who had died in war. He passed a shop on his way the elevator where Sarah Page was working.

How well these two knew one another has been a subject of great debates. Page had been working as an operator for six months. Rowland had been working as a shoe shiner for two years. At the very least they knew one another by sight. An exchange of words was probably common. But there is another theory.

In the 1970s, and again in the early 2000s, a family member of Rowland came forward and said that the two knew each other very well ind19eed. That the teenagers, one of whom was a girl running from a marriage and the other a boy of nineteen and all the ego and foolhardiness that comes with that age, were romantically involved. Aside from a few witness accounts, 50 years after the incident, there is absolutely nothing to support this theory. However, it is a theory that cannot be completely discounted.

Whether or not they were close, or barely acquaintances, Dick Rowland entered the elevator. Some sources claim that he tripped. Some say he jumped in. Most sources say that he grabbed her wrist. Page cried out. It could have been a cry of surprise at seeing her star-crossed beau unexpectedly. It could have been a cry of surprise at being grabbed while someone fell. It could have been a shout of fear, being a teenage girl who had been told most of her life that black men could not be trusted around white women. Maybe it was a gasp of shock at seeing someone she was acquainted with fall. As there are no surviving reports from her perspective it is impossible to tell.

Whatever the case, Dick Rowland ran. Did he run because Sarah Page cried out? Or because a clerk shouted at him? Again, we cannot know. Dick Rowland's account has not survived. He may have been a black man who was so overcome by Sarah Page that he tried to attack her in an elevator. Maybe they got into an argument because it was Memorial Day and no one really wanted to be working. He may have been a boy who tripped. He may have been a boy in love. Either way he ran. A clerk working at Renberg's, a clothing store, flagged down an officer and reported the crime.

The clerk told police that Page was in a "distressed state." This was enough for the cops to seek out Dick Rowland. Henry Carmichael and Henry C. Pack were the detective and the patrolman who tracked down and arrested Rowland. Carmichael was a white detective. Pack, however, was one of the two black patrolmen in Tulsa's law enforcement. They arrested Rowland who, according to reports, went with them without incident. Rowland was escorted to the Tulsa City Jailhouse.

As had happened in many other riots, newspapers and media played a large part in what would eventually occur.

The Tulda Tribune, a white, conservative newspaper with a flair for the sensationalist, ran the story of Rowland crime and capture just a few hours after his arrest. "Nab Nergro for Attacking Girl in an Elevator," the headline read. The entire article went on to sling misinformation.

"A negro delivery boy who gave his name to the public as "Diamond Dick" but who has been identified as Dick Rowland, was arrested on South Greenwood avenue this morning by Officers Carmichael and Pack, charged with attempting to assault the 17-year-old white elevator girl in the Drexel building early yesterday. He will be tried in municipal court

this afternoon on a state charge. The girl said she noticed the negro a few minutes before the attempted assault looking up and down the hallway on the third floor of the Drexel building as if to see if there was anyone in sight but thought nothing of it at the time. A few minutes later he entered the elevator she claimed, and attacked her, scratching her hands and face and tearing her clothes. Her screams brought a clerk from Renberg's store to her assistance and the negro fled. He was captured and identified this morning both by the girl and the clerk, police say. Tenants of the Drexel building said the girl is an orphan who works as an elevator operator to pay her way through business college."

The story ran on the front page. It fanned flames among the white Tulsa population. Here was yet another black man who was taking advantage of a poor white girl. Among blacks this was a prelude that had been read many times before.

According to some witnesses, this was not the only story to run in The Tribune about the incident. Another article, titled "To Lynch Negro Tonight," apparently ran in the paper, but the article has been lost. The page where this article is said to have run is missing from the Tribune's archives, including the microfilm copy. An intact copy of this article would be worth a great deal monetarily to the Tulsa Race Riot Archive. Other local papers did not write any articles in response to this alleged lynch-based article.

Police Commissioner J. M. Adkison received an anonymous phone call in the early afternoon. The exact phrase was not noted, but he says the phone call threatened the life of Rowland. The commissioner ordered that Rowland be moved to a more secure cell located at the top of the County Courthouse. On his way through the courthouse, Rowland was spotted by several lawyers. Due to his profession, he was well known to them. Later, they would tell papers that "I know that boy, and have known him a good while. That's not in him."

At 3 p.m. the "Nab Negro" story hit the streets. Rumors of a lynching began to spread through Tulsa. While many of Tulsa's citizens felt like justice was playing its course, after all the alleged assailant had already been caught and imprisoned, others felt like it was not enough. And, still others, worried that Dick Rowland would never get to tell his side of the events.

At sunset, several hundred white residents began to form outside of Tulsa's courthouse. The newly elected sheriff, Willard McCullough, wanted to keep things from getting out of hand. After all, he had been elected in place of the sheriff who had supported mob justice under the platform of doing good, law-abiding work. He assigned six officers to take up protective positions around Rowland. They were armed with rifles and shotguns. They moved Rowland to the roof and disabled the elevator, creating what protections they could.

Shortly after 8 p.m., three white men entered the courthouse and demanded that Rowland be turned over to them for the sake of justice. McCullough refused and told the mob to disband.

Three blocks away, in the Greenwood district, black men and women gathered at the Gurley Hotel. They worried that if a mob was willing to lynch a white boy of 19, what chance did a black boy of 19 have under the laws of segregation? There were arguments about what to do and how to handle things. Some, especially veterans, thought that fighting was the answer. Others felt that talking things out would work. Many believed that either way, they should make a showing at the courthouse, armed or not, to show Rowland that he was not alone.

One witness to the night's events claimed that McCollough invited the African American community to the courthouse. McCollough vehemently denied ever making this request, but it is part of a sworn statement in front of a grand jury by O. W. Gurley of the Gurley Hotel. Ten witnesses corroborated Gurley's statement.

Attorney James Luthor made the following statement:

"I saw a car full of negroes driving through the streets with guns; I saw Bill McCullough and told him those negroes would cause trouble; McCullough tried to talk to them, and they got out and stood in single file. W. G. Daggs was killed near Boulder and Sixth street. I was under the impression that a man with authority could have stopped and disarmed them. I saw Chief of Police on south side of court house on top step, talking; I did not see any officer except the Chief; I walked in the court house and met McCullough in about 15 feet of his door; I told him these negroes were going to make trouble, and he said he had told them to go home; he went out and told the whites to go home, and one said "they said you told them to come up here." McCullough said "I did not" and a negro said you did tell us to come."

Invited or not, 10 black men, most of them former World War I veterans, came to help guard Rowland. They arrived in a car, and they were armed.

This upset the mob of nearly 1,000 whites. Many went home to get their own guns. Members of the mob attempted to break into the National Guard Armory. However, Major Bell, who had heard of what was going on at the courthouse, had already taken preventative measures. He called up all local members of the Guard and had them arrive in uniform to protect the armory. When 300 men from the mob came with the intention of pillaging the guns and ammunition, Bell informed them that anyone who touched the building would be immediately shot by members of the National Guard. The mob sought arms elsewhere.

At the courthouse, John A. Gustafson attempted to talk the mob, who's numbers had swelled to 2,000, to go home. He was joined by several members of the clergy, including the first permanent pastor of Tulsa, Reverend Charles Kerr.

The former WWI veterans and other members of the Greenwood community got into two vehicles and moved them closer to the courthouse, in order to make a show of protection for Rowland.

The mob did not approve. In articles that would eventually be written, many mob members believed this protective action to be a preemptive uprising by the black community. Warning shots by the mob were fired into the air.

By 10 p.m., having not heard from the first group of 10, 75 more black men from Greenwood made for the courthouse to see what was going on. They saw over 2,000 white citizens gathered around, and feared for not only Rowland, but the original group. They approached McCullough, who told them that their help was not needed. The group of 75 gathered the group of 10 to talk with them and figure out what they were going to do next.

A white man told one of the black men to hand over his pistol. The black man refused. The white man reached for it.

It is unknown if the shot was accidental or on purpose. It could have been a warning shot. Either way, that shot, by a black man against a white one, set the fuse for the powder keg of Tulsa. The mob response was instantaneous. Within seconds, people were fighting. Using their World War I training, the Greenwood citizens fought an aggressive retreat, attempting to find a safe place to fall back to.

In this first fire fight, 10 whites and two blacks were killed.

The police force deputized a portion of the white men. According to the investigation, and confirmed by eyewitnesses, the deputies were told to "get a gun and get a nigger."

The white mob, now empowered by deputation, armed themselves with whatever they could, even stopping to loot stores for weapons. In the confusion, a third white man was shot by the mob. The riot was in full swing.

The National Guard, with help from the American Legion, began to patrol the streets. Their claim was that they were there to break up the mob, however, their only arrests were done against the black citizens of Greenwood, who they took to a local convention hall.

W. Tate Brady, a founder of Tulsa and a ranking KKK member, took up a leadership role among the mob. Brady was also accused of, but never arrested for, the tarring and feathering of the members of the IWW chapter in in 1917. It was his claim that tarring and feathering people was to protect the "women and children of Belgium," a popular phrase during and after World War I as Belgium had been invaded by Germany. Shouting it was a war cry against anything that was deemed unpatriotic, usually by members of KKK or similar groups. That was surprising, considering that Brady not only hired black workers at his businesses, but he married a Cherokee woman.

Brady led a group that attempted to take custody of Rowland shortly after 11 p.m. but was turned away by McCollough.

Gunfights took place on and off throughout the night. Predominately these fights took place around the courthouse, near the train tracks, and around the Greenwood district itself. Rumors began to crop up among the white mob that black reinforcements would use the train to come to Greenwood's aid. Train passengers were fired upon but not injured. In an effort to take ground, mob members used cars to cross the district lines and fired into any business and house in which they spotted movement, regardless of whether they were being fired upon first or not. Several Greenwood business owners fired back.

Just after 1 a.m. on June 1, four hours after the riot began, a group of white men who had crossed the district line walked down Archer street. They lit rags soaked in oil and used them to set fire to black-owned businesses, first targeting the ones whose citizens had fired back, and then others.

The Tulsa Fire Department scrambled, gathering to put out the blaze. The gathered mob members turned them away under threat of violence. Scott Ellsworth, a firefighter, spoke about that night several years after the fact. "It would mean a fireman's life to turn a stream of water on one of those negro buildings. They shot at us all morning when we were trying to do something but none of my men were hit. There is not a chance in the world to get through that mob into the negro district."

By 4 a.m. two dozen black businesses were on fire. Greenwood seemed to separate itself into two parts. The first part wanted to stay and protect what had been created. The other wanted to leave. Scores of Greenwood citizens used the nearby trains to leave the city. Other fought. Snipers, trained in war, took up positions within

Greenwood. Cars were moved to create barriers. Smoke and fire filled the air.

At 5 a.m. a siren, or perhaps a train whistle, sounded. The night was over, but the riot was not. Five white men got into a car and used it to rally other rioters. They used the car to propel themselves into the Greenwood district. They were gunned down before they made it a whole block. Angered, half of the mob, nearly 1,000 people, stormed in behind the car and overtook the neighborhood. Unable to fight against those numbers, the black citizens of Greenwood retreated to the edge of their district, the outskirts of Tulsa. Rioters, seeing this as a sign of absolute victory, went wild. They set fires, looted, and killed their way through what remained of Greenwood. Many were shot, some were beaten, several were lynched. Many broke into homes that had not participated in the riots at all and forced people into the streets to be arrested.

While Greenwood was the focus of the looting and rioting, it was not the only target. White homes that employed or housed black workers or tenants were also targeted. Rioters showed up at these homes, regardless of whether or not the African Americans within were participants, and demanded that they be turned over to white custody. Many complied. Those that did not were attacked, their homes vandalized.

The rioters believed that the Mount Zion Church, a historic landmark of Greenwood, was an armory that had received caskets full of weapons. Others claimed it was a fortress that was being used to "organize the negro forces."

The law officials and deputized rioters went to the nearby airfield and used privately owned planes to take to the skies. As few as six and as many as 13 planes circled the Greenwood District. Law enforcement said that it was for observation and recon against the "negro uprising," but several of these plans were used to firebomb the district. This forced old and young blacks, many who were taking cover during the riots, into the streets where they were then shot. There has been a great deal of controversy about this, as it would be the very first firebombing of America. Newspapers that came out shortly after the rioting say that the firebombing did not happen. However, history has shown that Tulsa World's articles from that time in history cannot be wholly trusted.

Beryl, a historian, has made the claim that the pictures of the burned-out buildings show that firebombs were not a possibility. If he is correct then Mount Zion and other parts of Greenwood were set ablaze on ground, rather than in the sky.

The fires continued later into the morning.

Around 9 a.m., Adjutant General Charles Barrett of the Oklahoma National Guard arrived by military train with 109 troops under the orders of the governor. By law he was required to make contact with local authorities, a difficult task since no one was entirely sure where authorities were. Barrett managed to find McCullough and the mayor, but not before he and his troops stopped to eat breakfast.

Deciding that the task was too much for his forces, Barrett requested reinforcements from other parts of Oklahoma. The governor established martial law at 11:49 am. Between 4,000 and 6,000 black men, women, and children were interred at the Convention Hall, the Tulsa Fairgrounds, or McNulty Park.

The rioters and the Greenwood residents were not pleased with the Nation Guard's presence. Both sides fired on them. Martial law officially ended on June 4, 1921.

CHAPTER NINE

AFTERMATH

———————————◆———————————

The face of Tulsa, Oklahoma, changed in the days, weeks, months, and even years following the massacre. By land and by air 35 blocks of property were burned and destroyed. Eight hundred people were hospitalized. Six thousand were interred or arrested. Many of those who were interred, six thousand of them were put on trains to be sent to other parts of the country to live. According to the Oklahoma Bureau of Vital Statistics, at least 36 died, 26 of whom were black and 10 who were white. The Commission of Tulsa claimed that death tolls were likely near 400 dead, 300 black and 100 white. The Red Cross decided that due to the amount of people who had been sent on trains and a lack of organization in the hours during and directly after the massacre that an exact number was impossible.

Real estate valuing $1.5 million (the equivalent of $31.1 million today) was lost on the night of May 30. Destroyed personal property totaled $750,000, or almost $10 million in current dollars. The Black Wall Street, a culmination of the work of thousands, was obliterated and it would never really return.

City planners rezoned the Greenwood district as industrial and made plans to build over it with white-owned factories and businesses. The Tulsa World said that black community leaders O.W. Gurley, Rev. H.T.F. Johnson and Barney Cleaver did not have a "note of dissension" about the idea. Not surprising considering that Tulsa World, whose prose played a huge factor in the start of the riot, also claimed that everything started because the black community was attempting to aggressively take over Tulsa for union and Marxist ideals.

The committee agreed that Greenwood was lost, and promises were made for the city to pay for the land that had been lost. In some circumstances this was carried out. In others it was not. White looters, who claimed that they had earned the land, refused to give up the area that they had taken by force. They were pushed out by law enforcement.

A grand jury was called together to decide who had done wrong, and what exactly they had done. This process would be repeated in 1996 and again in 2001. The decision made by the later bipartisan committees and the historians who helped piece together accounts from eye witnesses, articles, and pictures, was that the Tulsa Race Massacre happened because of a certain lackadaisical lawlessness that allowed for a second rise of the KKK. That long-term tensions between wealthy blacks who were becoming wealthier, and labor unions who were fighting to get pay reached a boiling point, though the fire had been set by elite whites and newspapers who cared more about a political agenda that expressing the facts.

The fact is that the incident that acted as a catalyst was rooted in misinformation.

Sarah Page, who left Tulsa less than a week after the riots, never pressed charges. In fact, before leaving, she asked that all charges be dropped. The case against Dick Rowland fell apart. In September, Rowland was completely exonerated of all the charges against him. He left Tulsa.

Millions of dollars in property damage, mass unmarked graves, families split by death and forced transportation, and the only firebombs dropped on America by Americans all happened because a boy most likely tripped while getting on an elevator and he happened to be black when it happened. While years of hatred, yellow journalism, of romanticizing vigilantism, and a lack of organized law enforcement played a part, ultimately it was Dick Rowland tripping over his own feet that caused years of simmering hatreds to play out what many have deemed inevitable.

In Tulsa, a committee against racial violence was formed. It was made up of 250 white citizens. When the story of Tulsa eventually vanished from newspapers, and the grand jury made its choices, Tulsa decided not to speak much of the incident until 1996. Ten years later it was added to the school curriculum. Memorials were put up.

They attempted to file for these reparations that were promised during the committee that decided to turn Greenwood into an industrial zone. Oklahoma decided that the Statute of Limitations had expired and as of 2018 not a single black citizen of the Tulsa Massacre has received reparations from what happened that night. As of this writing, 97 of them are still alive.

CPSIA information can be obtained
at www.ICGtesting.com
Printed in the USA
BVHW032144051121
620957BV00012B/153